TRENDS IN RARE BOOKS AND DOCUMENTS SPECIAL COLLECTIONS MANAGEMENT, 2013 EDITION

By James Moses

ISBN: 978-1-57440-226-1
Library of Congress Control Number: 2013933870
©2013 Primary Research Group, Inc.

TABLE OF CONTENTS

TABLE OF CONTENTS 3
BOSTON PUBLIC LIBRARY 5
   The BPL Rare Book Collection 5
   Cataloging 6
   Digitization Lab 6
   Exhibits 7
   Collection Security 7
   Public Programming 8
   Online Efforts & Digitization Plans 8
   Sales of Prints 9
   Digital Repository 9
   Funding 10
   Manuscript Collection Finding Aids 10
ABE BOOKS 12
   Brief History 12
   Abe Books Website as an Industry Resource 13
   The Abe Books Business Model 15
   How Libraries Use the Abe Books Site 16
   Some Recent Books Featured on the Abe Website 17
UNIVERSITY OF ILLINOIS AT URBANA-CHAMPAIGN 20
   Sources of Funding 20
   Public Programming 21
   Midwest Book and Manuscript Studies Program 22
   Digitization Efforts 23
   Cataloging 23
   Relationship with The Library Science School 24
   BiblioTECH 25
   Exhibits 26
   Security & Theft 26
WASHINGTON UNIVERSITY OF ST. LOUIS 27
   Cooperation with the Art Department 27
   Specialization in British Fine Arts Presses 28
   Endowments 28
   Users of the Rare Book Collection 28
   Security 29
   Acquisitions 29
   Public Programs 29
   Collaborations 30
   Using the Collection for Educational Purposes 30
   Exhibits 30
   Fundraising 30
   Best Practices 31

ARCHIVES AND RARE BOOKS LIBRARY, UNIVERSITY OF CINCINNATI 32
General Description 32
Acquisitions and Development 34
Security and Theft 35
Digitization 36
Outreach and Publicity 37
Exhibits 39
Preservation 39

RARE BOOKS AND MANUSCRIPT LIBRARY AT THE OHIO STATE UNIVERSITY 41
General Description 41
Acquisitions and Development 43
Security and Theft 45
Digitization 46
Outreach and Publicity 47
Exhibits 48
Preservation 49

MANUSCRIPTS, ARCHIVES, AND RARE BOOK LIBRARY (MARBL), EMORY UNIVERSITY 51
General Description 51
Acquisitions and Development 53
Security and Theft 54
Digitization 54
Outreach and Publicity 56
Exhibits 58
Preservation 59

A POSTSCRIPT ON THE EFFORTS OF LAW ENFORCEMENT AGENCIES IN COMBATING RARE BOOK AND DOCUMENT THEFT 60

BOSTON PUBLIC LIBRARY

We interviewed Ms. Susan Glover, Keeper of Special Collections for the Boston Public Library.

The BPL Rare Book Collection

The BPL's rare book collection is perhaps best known for its American Revolutionary War and anti-slavery materials (Boston was a hotbed of the Abolitionist Movement), as well as for its extensive collection on the famous (some would say infamous) Sacco Vanzetti trial in the 1920's. Some leading books and documents from the collection include John Adam's Boston Massacre Trial Notes, the Sacco Vanzetti Collection, and two copies of the Bay Sound Book the first book written and printed in Colonial America. Glover says that the most popular collection is its anti-slavery collection which features more than 60,000 books and manuscripts featuring works by William Lloyd Garrison, editor of the Liberator, and a key figure in the abolitionist movement. Other leading collections include the Ticknor Collection of Spanish and Portuguese Literature, mostly from the Golden Age of Iberian Literature in the 17th century, including a first edition of Cervantes" Don Quixote. The BPL also has an extensive Shakespeare collection and a "huge theater collection" especially focused on theater in Boston.

Overall, the collection has more than 500,000 volumes and 1,000,000 manuscripts. The multi-media conscious BPL also offers a sound archive, for both musical recording, oral histories and other sound-based intellectual property, as well as video files for download, as well as an array of photographs, posters, prints and other visual artwork.

The BPL recently received a 3 year grant from the Boston Foundation, a local benefactor, to conserve, digitize and catalog the Library's anti-slavery collection. "We are in the process of digitizing all of the manuscripts in the anti-slavery collection," says Glover.

Cataloging

Glover laments the loss of the Library's curator of rare books, a position that was lost in a round of local government budget cutting. Now, rare book cataloging starts in the library's main copy cataloging center and then moves to the rare books department where Glover admits she sometimes does the nitty-gritty work herself. She hopes that the BPL can soon fund a rare books cataloger.

Digitization Lab

The BPL has a digitization lab that does digitization work for the entire library. The state of the art lab was started five years ago and receives what Glover calls generous funding from the city of Boston. The lab is part of the library's technical services department, and has its own full and part time staff. The BPL also partners with the Internet Archives, and is one of its scanning sites.

Exhibits

The BPL uses the lobby of the rare books department for exhibit space and has been holding 3 exhibits per year. As the Library moves ahead with its ambitious rare book digitization schedule, Glover believes that the emphasis may shift somewhat to online exhibits. The BPL rare books department is an active lender to other libraries and to museums and recently has contributed to exhibits at Tufts University, The Folger, Boston College, The Hillwood Museum, Philadelphia Museum of Art, and The National Museum of Jewish-American History."

Collection Security

The Boston Public Library was one of the libraries victimized by the infamous thief E Forbes Smiley. After the crimes of this notorious thief (who also victimized Harvard, Yale, the NY Public Library, and others) came to light, the BPL undertook a thorough security audit and altered some of its security procedures. "We have someone acting as a security person in the reading room at all times and we have cameras with a direct feed to the Boston Police Department. We have not had any further incidents, she notes but adds, "We are always vigilant about security I am happy with what we have but I am always vigilant."

Glover also notes that "We are in the middle of the building but if you have devious intentions it would be difficult to get in and out. We have someone acting as a security person in the reading room at all times. The reading room is staffed at all times and we have cameras with direct feed to the Boston Police Department." She notes that other security features are in place that she declined to identify.

Public Programming

Boston is a city full of higher education institutions and Glover says that the BPL has forged relationships with many of them to use the rare books collection in their courses. "Most regular arrangements, and there are quite a few, come about informally when a professor is using one of the BPL collections in the course of academic research. Simmons College (which has a major library science graduate program) comes in to teach a course based on our medieval manuscripts and we have a grad English course from UMASS (University of Massachusetts) come in every year. We have a great 19th century literature collection and a great Daniel Defoe collection. The Art Institute of Boston uses our art books and books on the history of typography. We have a strong incunabula collection (books printed between 1445 and Jan 1, 1501), books from the pioneer years of movable type, literally books 'in the cradle.'"

Online Efforts & Digitization Plans

The BPL is quite ambitious in its online portrayal efforts. For example its extensive collection of US War Posters, Art Posters, and Historic Photographs, thousands of items, can be accessed online through Yahoo Flickr. An extensive array of enormously interesting historic materials can be viewed and often reproduced and ordered through the BPL's extensive online store. The Flickr library also includes many photographs of local popular interest such as historic photographs of the Boston Celtics (basketball team) and the Boston Bruins (hockey team) as well as stirring and disturbing photographs from the Great Boston Fire of 1872, and photos of the Bunker Hill Memorial and other events, monuments and themes in Boston History. This adroitly chosen and well presented archive assures strong local interest in the collections and helps as an entry point to encourage browsing beyond the familiar.

Glover says that the BPL rare books department has aggressive digitization plans. "We really are focusing a lot on our digital effort and we are open 9-5 but as we digitize we are breaking those barriers of time and space. The more we digitize the more people come to see the real thing – there was always this idea that when you put it online you would put it in storage you would never use it again but the opposite happens – the digitization increases use of these collections and not decreasing it."

Sales of Prints

The BPL allows downloads from its site for all photos, prints, paintings and other visual resources that are in the public domain (everything on the Flickr site is in the public domain), and will even send recipients, who need not have a library card from the Boston Public Library, high resolution files suitable for printing. Glover says, "We get huge numbers of requests for prints, especially some of the photos of Boston history."

Digital Repository

The Boston Public Library is developing its own digital repository which it expects to have up and running in the next year. Glover feels that the repository will enhance the

Library's capabilities in exhibiting and otherwise offering its rare book collection online. The Library will still probably maintain its other online distribution sites for its online collection, such as its Flickr site, since they have a highly developed audience.

Funding

Initially, much of the collection came from Bostonian captains of industry in the 19th and early 20th century but, even more than these original and substantial contributions, the BPL rare books department acquisition effort is sustained by an enviable network of endowments. The rare books department acquisition efforts are not supported by taxpayer dollars, though salaries in the division are government supported. The BPL rare books department enjoys the fruits of more than 25 endowments, many earmarked for special types of rare books, or by subject matter. Some of the BPL rare book department's endowments are: The Artz Fund, focused on Longfellow, a fund for its Sacco Vanzetti Collection, another for rare books and manuscripts of a "military or patriotic" character, and another for Boston History. Others include a fund for books and manuscripts about world fairs, and a theater books fund.

Manuscript Collection Finding Aids

The BPL is enthusiastic in developing finding aids for its collections and the Rare Book and Manuscripts Department has developed an aid called Creators, which can be found on the BPL website. Creators is an alphabetical finding aid that enables scholars to search the BPL collection by collection type, creator or subject. "It gives you images, abstract, provenance, detailed descriptions; we started this last year. Scholars use it since we get requests based on what they learn in the online finding aids; it has all the info you would find in a print finding aid but it is online. This is a wonderful thing for scholars. What we are tying to do is to get the finding aid info out there so that they can ask for specific parts of the collection in advance. We are using software called ARCHON – an open source program so it costs noting in hard dollars but it costs a lot in staff time. But it is certainly worth it – this program spoke to our needs and we got it from the University of Illinois, and it is widely used."

ABE BOOKS

Abe Books is one of the premier websites for the online buying and selling of rare books and documents, competing with companies such as eBay, Alibris, Biblio and others. We interviewed Richard Davies, public relations manager for Abe Books.

Brief History

As described in its informative website, "Abe Books is an online marketplace for books." Perhaps more than many other online bookstores, Abe Books has carved out a niche for itself in rare and antiquarian book sales. If you were wondering how it competes with the online giant of global online book purchasing, Amazon.com, it doesn't, since Amazon purchased Abe Books in 2008 and Abe is now a subsidiary of Amazon, though its website is still unimpeachably its own. While Abe Books is perhaps best known in the rare and antiquarian book market, it is also active in the general used book industry and especially in college textbooks where it is a well known major player.

Founded in Canada in 1996 and active in the North American market from inception, Abe Books expanded internationally into Europe ten years ago with sites for the UK and France, and it also purchased a German provider in the same industry. Five years ago it launched in Italy. In response to our query Davies says that the company has no current plans to expand in Asia, citing the very low book prices in Asia and the difficulties of working in less familiar Asian languages.

Abe, with headquarters in Victoria, Canada, Abe currently maintains six international sites – AbeBooks.com, AbeBooks.co.uk, AbeBooks.de, AbeBooks.fr, AbeBooks.it, IberLibro.com, and ZVAB.com – and offers the well followed rare book blog, http://www.abebooks.com/blog.

Abe Books Website as an Industry Resource

Like its parent Amazon, Abe Books is primarily a technology company that uses computing power to illuminate and makes accessible the pleasures of used and rare books. Whether you sell of buy on the site, or neither, the Abe site is a useful resource for library rare book collections and a trove of information and marketing savvy.

Among the irresistible nuggets of information for rare-book-aholics offered on this useful site is a list of rare-book related blogs which we reproduce below:

- Bibliodyssey
- Book Patrol
- Book Trout
- BookFinder.com
- BookForum
- Bookgasm
- Bookplate Junkie
- Bookride
- Books, Inq
- Bookslut

- Brain Pickings
- Edward Champion's Return of the Reluctant
- Fine Books & Collections
- Galley Cat
- Guardian Book Blog
- Jacket Copy
- LibraryThing
- Literary Saloon
- Melville House Publishing Blog
- Omnivoracious
- Page-Turner: The New Yorker Book Blog
- Paris Review Blog
- Ready Steady Book
- Shelf:Life
- The Millions

The site also offers a list of monthly "Most Expensive Sales" and an archive of such sales going back 3 or 4 years. So the site provides sufficient information to get some idea of recent price trends, at least for the most expensive rare books.

In addition, the site offers a truly stunning array of content that we feel can inspire rare book departments to fire up campus or library patron interest in their own collections. Abe Books, in the true Amazon, or perhaps also the true Abe Books tradition, uses content to inspire interest in content, and for rare book collections, not always best known for their marketing abilities or emphasis on what might be called promotion, this is truly a useful service.

The content on the site is delivered in article-length features such as "Collecting Civil War Books" which feature historical notes and the appealing presentation of some interesting titles such as *The Spy of the Rebellion* by Allan Pinkerton, who headed the Union spy effort and later the famed Pinkerton Detective Agency. Other articles include: "*Collecting Rare Cookbooks*" and "*Books Signed by Movie Stars*" or "*Britain in Picture.*" These are presentations that would kindle interest from anyone who might have previously looked upon the world of rare books as the exclusive preserve of eccentric librarians. They bring the panache of the major museum to the world of rare books, a panache that could be useful to library rare book collections looking for marketing skills.

The Abe Books Business Model

The company is an online marketplace for buyers and sellers and does not itself maintain book stocks or inventory. Its business model is to take a percentage of each sale (13.5% in most cases) from the seller; the buyer pays no fees. In addition, sellers are required to pay a modest base fee (starting at $25 per month to list up to 500 titles) to list on the site. Davies says that one of the reasons for the fee is to essentially weed out sellers who are not really serious long term sellers of rare books and documents. The site caters to private collectors, university and related collections, bookstores and book wholesalers as well as some publishers, rather than to casual sellers. The monthly fee rises to as much as $500 per month for those organizations listing more than 500,000 titles.

How Libraries Use the Abe Books Site

Davies says that many university and other library collections use the site, primarily as buyers, but occasionally as sellers. He says that public libraries, particularly through Friends of the Library organizations, often sell on the site and a few libraries have sellers' accounts.

For the most part, as might be expected, the library rare book collections are buyers, and Davies points to a unique and highly useful feature of the Abe website that he says collections and library collections make use of extensively. The service is called WANTS and though it a customer can list characteristics of the book or type of books he is looking for, defined by author, title, publication date range, price and innumerable other variables, and have an email alert sent to him when a title that fits the chosen parameters is up for sale on Abe Books. So, for example, a university collection focused on early 20th century American drama might want to be alerted on all Eugene O'Neill scripts published between 1905 and 1925. Or a collector focused on first editions of American writers might tag "Mark Twain" and "first edition" and be alerted when any new first editions of Mark Twain novels hit the website. Davies says that the feature is perfect for special collections that are only interested in purchasing very specific items that fit their mandate, price level and collection criteria.

Davies also points to another area of the site often useful for collectors. It is called Book Sleuth. Davies explains: "if you can't remember the name of a title exactly you can go to the forums (and seek help) and describe what the book looks like, or describe the story – and then they post their answers – this is a super useful community tool."

Some Recent Books Featured on the Abe Website

1. Mystere de la Vengeance de Notre Seigneur by Eustache Mercade - $20,000

Published in 1491 in Paris by Antoine Verard, this first edition lacks 16 leaves, but only one complete copy is known to exist, in the Bibliotheque Nationale in Paris. The sale also included a letter by French bibliographer Amedee Boinet, who confirms the exceptional rarity of this book.

2. A 13th century Latin bible – $19,314

Written on vellum and produced in Paris around 1250. A beautiful handwritten manuscript with decorations in the margins and initials in red and blue. Rebound with 16th century leather with one remaining clasp.

3. The Old Man and the Sea by Ernest Hemingway - $18,500

Published in 1952, this first edition was inscribed by the author "with very best wishes, Ernest Hemingway, Keywest/1958."

4. The Savoy Cocktail Book by Harry Craddock - $9,500

A first edition, published in 1930 by Constable & Company, Ltd, of this famous Art Deco cocktail book. The book was inscribed "Here's How! 'Harry Craddock'/ 'To Bert' October 12, '31." Bound in burgundy morocco by the famous English bookbinders Sangorski & Sutcliffe.

5. The Age of Innocence by Edith Wharton - $9,000

First edition, first printing published in 1920 by Appleton. The first issue dust jacket had been professionally restored.

6. Notes on the Colors of the National Guard, with some Incidental Passages of the History of the Regiment - $8,000

An American civil war regimental history of the 7th New York National Guard; limited issue (three of 67) published in 1864. Illustrated with 15 mounted albumen photographs of veterans, and numerous patriotic vignettes within the text.

7. The Wheel of Time Series by Robert Jordan - $7,000

A set of 12 books - all signed first editions from Jordan's Wheel of Time series - The Eye if the World, The Great Hunt, The Dragon Reborn, The Shadow Rising, The Fires of Heaven, Lord of Chaos, A Crown of Swords, The Path of Daggers, Winter's Heart, Crossroads of Twilight, Knife of Dreams and The Gathering Storm.

8. L' Art du Trait de Charpenterie par le Sieur Nicolas Fourneau, Maitre Charpentier Rouen, Ci-Devant Conducteur de Charpente et Démonstrateur du Trait à Paris by Nicholas Fourneaux -$6,666

Published in four parts between 1767 and 1772, and bound in two uniform red half leather bindings. An extremely rare complete set of first editions. In the first three books Fourneaux describes methods to calculate and design complex carpentry and woodwork. The fourth part deals almost exclusively with geometry and projection.

9. Les Illustrations de Gaule et Singularitez de Troye, par Maistre Jean Le Maire de Belges, avec la Couronne Margaritique et Plusieurs Autres Oeuvres de luy, non Jamais Encore Imprimées by Jean Lemaire de Belges - $6280

A retelling of the Trojan legend, illustrated by Jean Lemaire de Belges, published in 1549.

10. De la Puissance légitime du Prince sur le Peuple, et du Peuple sur le Prince by Hubert Languet and Philippe de Mornay - $6,162

Originally written in Latin by Estienne Junius Brutus and translated later into this first French edition in the late 16th century, this book discusses individual freedom and the rights of peoples against royalty.

UNIVERSITY OF ILLINOIS AT URBANA-CHAMPAIGN

The University of Illinois at Urbana-Champaign boasts a rare book collection of ½ million volumes. Led by its enthusiastic chairwoman Valerie Hotchkiss, its highly involved and creative rare books team is anxious to use a museum management style to boost the presence and impact of its rare book collections in university life and beyond.

Sources of Funding

Although the department has what Hotchkiss regards as a pitifully small staff of 6 FTE, plus student help equal to roughly another 1.5 FTE, Hotchkiss' energetic vision is made somewhat easier by the existence of 12 special endowments for rare books. We asked Hotchkiss how her department had managed such a feat and she said that donors were often highly interested in rare books, which have a tangible and scholarly quality, and that rare book collections can benefit by asserting themselves in the pursuit of endowments, both of their own accord, and through the advancement efforts of the general university. "Special collections departments pretty much sell themselves to potential donors," says Hotchkiss.

Hotchkiss says that some of the endowments are targeted. For example, one is for rare art books, and another for books on cows and horses, but all allow flexibility in spending. Unlike budgetary funds, endowment funds accumulate year to year and are not lost if not spent.

Public Programming

The department is aided in its fundraising efforts by a steadfastly presented series of public programs aimed at raising the profile of the rare books division and engaging the rest of the university and the public at large. "We taught 201 classes in rare books and manuscripts last year," says Hotchkiss, who elaborates "these are seminars in the university, for graduate students in history or medieval studies, religious studies, math and other fields (in addition to library science). The rare books department provides one or two sessions in their course. We work with faculty so that they can integrate use of the rare book collection into their courses. We actually give prizes each year, one for graduate students and one for undergrads, for the paper that makes the best use of our primary sources."

In addition to encouraging use of the collection in coursework, the department also held 28 public programs (exhibits, lectures, workshops, plays, concerts and other performances, etc) in the past year with an aggregated total attendance of more than 2,000. "For example," explains Hotchkiss, "we had an evening showing of a new documentary film on Carl Sandburg. We have Carl Sandburg's papers here and much of the research for the documentary was done here. We had a Dickensian reading circle where a group of 20 people came in to read all of Dickens' Christmas Carols aloud and we had a special St. Valentine's Day lecture on the true history of St. Valentine's Day, which is quite bookish."

Public programming is also aimed at local K-12 education. "We are not afraid of children here," says Hotchkiss. "We did a special opening for children on Aesop, and we bring in high school students for their English and history classes and then we register them (the high school not the grade school students) so that they can (independently of the particular program) use the collection."

The public performances help the rare books division to reach out to new constituencies, such as the performing arts community. "We performed a lost play by Mark Twain; the play is called *Is he Dead Yet*? This year we will be performing a play by Dickens and Wilkie Collins – *The Frozen Deep* – and we will perform it on Charles Dickens birthday and there will be an exhibit on the Arctic at that time. My basic philosophy is to make sure we do something to keep what is in our books alive on our campus. Rare book & manuscripts libraries will survive but we won't do ourselves any favors unless we embrace a museum model and get out there and keep the ideas that are in our books alive – in front of all kinds of people, old people, young people, kids, faculty, and the local community."

Midwest Book and Manuscript Studies Program

The Rare Books division is also well integrated with Urbana's well known School of Library Science through its Midwest Book and Manuscript Studies Program, which can be a stand alone certificate, or part of the broader Masters of Library Science degree program of the School of Library Science. This certificate program, also available through online courses, is of greater and greater interest to the library science community, says Hotchkiss. "As the book dies interest in the study of the rare book as a cultural and physical object is becoming stronger and stronger," she says.

The University of Illinois at Urbana-Champaign has what many regard as the leading library science graduate school in the USA, and the rare books department has much interaction and collaborative activity with it.

Digitization Efforts

Hotchkiss says online exhibits reach many more people than in-house exhibits and that the Department is now putting a greater emphasis on them. The Rare Books Division makes use of a library wide digitization center but also has fond the funds to develop its own rare book study technology center (for digitization among other applications) that is calls BiblioTECH. The center, which is directed by a full time staffer, and also enjoys some graduate student support from the library science program, initially cost $50,000 to set up, exclusive of the costs of physical space. The funds were used to purchase computer, cameras, screens and other equipment.

Cataloging

Hotchkiss says that the rare books department puts a great emphasis on proper cataloging. "We don't digitize here unless we properly catalog. There are multiple access points to any digitized piece that we do. When I first came we have a backlog or hidden collections – we had over 70,000 un-cataloged books including a first folio of William Shakespeare so we got a Mellon grant 4 years ago and used it to hire a project leader, a recent graduate from the University library science program. That person has been training grad students in library and info science who have had two cataloging classes and they come here as hourly employees and they learn the nuts and bolts of rare book cataloging. Most do it for about 6-9 months and then they are trained as really good rare book catalogers. We do not give the books a Dewey number we use an Accession number like a museum would use so they sit on the shelves – it gives you a record. They have done over 70,000 books in 4 years. We catalog them at a cost of $11 to $16 for title – they claim in our cataloging department that it cost $25. We have placed students at MIT, the Library of Congress, and University of Edinburgh. All of our procedures, our policies, our workflow it is all up online – quick and clean."

Relationship with The Library Science School

The rare books department is intimately involved in education efforts directed at the library science profession as a whole.

"We run the Midwest Book and Manuscript Studies Program and it is a certificate program – it can stand alone or it is offered with the library science school. Many of the classes are offered online – one I give tomorrow on online presentation. We have enough classes online so that you can get a certificate online. We encourage hands on learning – we do encourage students to get to a library and do an internship, 40% of the incoming class is interested in this program. As the book dies the study of the rare book as a cultural object and physical object is becoming stronger and stronger."

BiblioTECH

Urbana has recently inaugurated a center called BiblioTECH. "That is where we recognize and make use of new technologies to study rare books and manuscripts," says Hotchkiss. The center was initially established with a $50,000 grant for cameras, screens and computers, she says, adding "I also begged and pleaded for some extra space." The center is staffed with a director and one staff member and Hotchkiss sees BiblioTech as a step beyond more traditional, if this word can be used, library digitization centers.

"BiblioTech is not just digitization – there is a digitization lab here in the library but they do the digitization but then we do the manipulation of data and the cataloging here," she explains: "We are trying to do more with digitization – we try to capture the physical anatomy of the book." Another emphasis is on proper cataloging. "We don't digitize here unless we properly catalog it. There are multiple access points to get to any digitized piece that we do."

Hotchkiss emphasizes that rare book collections must use the entire resources of the great universities in which they are often spawned, commenting on her own division's efforts:

"We work with computer scientists to read handwriting. We work with spectral analysis – using a range of lights but because we are at a huge university we think: why not work with the scientists? We try to make the best use of our location in a great university and we have a lot of collaborations with people."

Exhibits

Hotchkiss is dissatisfied with the exhibition space available to the collection, noting that "this is one of the top ten collections in the country and we are in a little wing of the main library. We have no exhibition space; we need an exhibition hall, so we do traveling exhibits. We are sitting here in the cornfields so we have to get things out. We have exhibits in Frankfurt and we have lent to many institutions. We cannot bring traveling exhibitions in here since we can't pass the American Museum standards."

Security & Theft

Hotchkiss says that in the early 1970's there was a theft of an important book but since then there have not been any problems. "We have a really good security system now with cameras and bio-readers." She feels one of the real problems with the rising concerns among rare book librarians with theft is its impact on apprenticeships. "The apprenticeship model is the most important way to train people – some rare book libraries will shun volunteers for the possible security threat," she says.

WASHINGTON UNIVERSITY OF ST. LOUIS

The Rare Books Department is housed in the Library's department of special collections, headed by Anne Marie Posega, whom we interviewed. The Library's special collections department has approximately 56,000 rare books and the University also houses additional rare books in the East Asian, Medical and other libraries on campus. The Rare Books unit has a curator and an assistant.

Cooperation with the Art Department

Rare Books extensively collaborates with the University's Department of Fine Arts. The two departments jointly run what it calls The Book Studio, a production facility for the maintenance, repair and creation of books. The Studio, which was initially jointly funded by the Library, the Fine Arts Department, and a donor, is jointly controlled by the two departments though day to day financing is under the Fine Arts Department, and the facility is housed at the school of Art. Various classes are taught in the book studio relating to book production and graphic design.

The Fine Arts Department has "a very strong graphics program" says Posega and its students are the primary users of the Book Studio which has a broad range of presses, reproduction and archival equipment, among other assets.

The Fine Arts Department is one of the most extensive end users of the rare book collection. The two departments are also collaborating on a digitization program called

Urban Books. "It is comprised of contemporary artists' books that focus on urban themes."

Specialization in British Fine Arts Presses

The heart of the Washington University collection is a complete collection of all of the works of three British fine arts presses – Dove Press, Kelmscott, and Ashendene. The Library has all of the books of these renowned publishers starting with their initial works in the 1890s. Other areas of significant strength include semiology, encompassing the history of communications, cryptology and universal languages, among other topics.

Endowments

Rare books has five endowments, including one fund for pre-1800 British and European books and maps and other printed items, called The Grossman Endowment.

Users of the Rare Book Collection

Posega believes that art students account for more than two thirds of the use of the rare book collection. Rare books have been extensively worked into the art department's curriculum, though other departments such as History, English, and Romance Languages are also more than casual users. In addition to use by its own students and faculty, Rare Books is a resource for other local colleges and occasionally for high schools. Rare Books has also collaborated with the St. Louis Public Library and made extensive collection loans to Monticello and other museums and universities where rare books are exhibited.

Security

Posega says that the department has good security and has not had issues with theft. "The building was remodeled in 2004 and so we have the opportunity to redesign the room so that all the end users are visible from the front desk and we have the usual cameras and door alarms, and glass shatter alarms – that kind of thing," Posega points out.

Acquisitions

The endowment funds earmarked for rare books account for most of the purchasing budget which is also supplemented by gifts. The Department maintains regular relationships with dealers "who know the areas we collect in and so they will contact us with things that interest us," explains Posega. Donated collections are also an important source. "We are getting a significant collection of miniature books right now. They are classified by height- the maximum is no more than 3 inches in height or thickness. The donor is also providing upkeep money."

Public Programs

The Division has "a pretty active schedule of public programs," and Posega says one of the most popular events is a favorite books series where a faculty member or student will give a talk on a book in the collection that they have worked with. "We have two to six of those a year and we also have a lecture on the history of books or printing each year."

Collaborations

Rare Books collaborates extensively with local institutions and has co-sponsored panel discussions at the Missouri History Museum and has loaned aspects of its collection to Monticello and the St. Louis Art Museum.

Using the Collection for Educational Purposes

"Of the five units in special collections, Rare Books is the one most used by faculty mostly because the art program is such a heavy user of the art collection – they probably do at least seventy percent of the use but we also get used by History, English and Romance Languages, among others. We also get use by other colleges in the area particularly for the book arts collection; there are faculty at other schools who have been bringing in classes for years. We have collaborated with the St. Louis Public Library and get some interest from high school classes that come in."

Exhibits

Rare Books has use of exhibition space in the main library that is shared by all special collections units. "Sometimes we will have a joint exhibit from several units. We do have digital exhibits as well: one we had recently is related to the Jefferson books we hold."

Fundraising

Special Collections works closely with the University's Development Office to raise money, and Development has assigned a specific person from the office to work with the

Library. Events are also an important means of making contacts to raise money, since 99% of the Library's special events (many of which involve special collections and particularly rare books) are open to the public. The Library also has a special program that raises money specifically for book conservation called Legacy of Books though which donors can give small amounts.

"There is a brochure and this gets mailed out to library supporters and our development officer can sometimes mail to other university mailing lists and it is on the library website. We have gotten some large donations of a thousand and up and then some for hundreds of dollars and we use these funds for special boxes."

Best Practices

Posega feels that: "Our favorite book series has been a good idea, especially if there is a faculty member giving the talk and then other faculty see what use the collection has been, and I think our collaboration with the School of Art has been very good for both partners."

ARCHIVES AND RARE BOOKS LIBRARY, UNIVERSITY OF CINCINNATI

We spoke with Kevin Grace, Head of the Archives and Rare Books Library at the University of Cincinnati. Mr. Grace has been with the library for thirty-three years. He is also the University Archivist.

General Description

The Archives and Rare Books Library at the University of Cincinnati is one of twelve libraries in the UC library system. Since its founding in 1975, the collection has been housed in Blegen Library on the main campus, one of three libraries to call Blegen its home. "We occupy essentially five floors," Mr. Grace explains, making it the largest of the three libraries in the facility: the Albino Gorno Memorial Music Library takes up two floors, while the John Miller Burnam Classical Library lays claim to four floors. Prior to its establishment in a dedicated space in 1975, the rare books collection was integrated as part of the general library, dating back to the university's founding in 1819.

Boasting a collection of 38,000 total volumes and approximately 35,000 linear feet of archival materials, the Archives and Rare Books Library covers an immense range, from early manuscripts to modern first editions. Of particular significance is the library's German-Americana Collection. "It probably doesn't get the most use," admits Mr. Grace, "but it is the most well known, internationally, and it is what sets us apart." Founded on the private library of German-American educator and writer H.H. Fick, the collection is one of the nation's largest collection of books, manuscripts, and journals focusing on German-American literature, history, and culture, totaling an estimated 5,000 volumes in all. "The depth of the material really reflects the Ohio Valley," says Mr. Grace. World War I anti-German hysteria saw the region rejecting its German heritage. "German language programs in public schools were cut. But [Fick] continued collecting, up until his death." Obtained by the University of Cincinnati library in 1935 (after Fick's death), the collection became a part of the general UC libraries—where it remained until 1974, when it was officially organized as the German-Americana Collection.

While the Fick Collection may garner the most attention, Mr. Grace cites the Rare Books Collection and the University Archives as the two that see the most use. Regarding the Rare Books Collection, Mr. Grace lists 18th century British literature as a strength, along with the history of the book, North American Indians, and early travel and exploration. Irish literature (both contemporary and dating back to the 18th century) is an asset, and Rare Books Collection also houses a great deal of Charles Dickens materials, including first issues and first editions. Materials focusing on the Arts & Crafts Movement have seen increased use over the past few years.

In addition to these popular collections, the Archives and Rare Books Library houses the holdings of local government records, known as the Ohio Network Collection, covering eight southwestern Ohio counties and municipalities. Highlights of these holdings include nearly 530,000 Cincinnati birth and death records, Hamilton County citizenship records from 1837 to 1916, and Hamilton County wills filed between 1791 and 1901. Mr. Grace also points to the library's Urban Studies Collection as a strong suit. This collection chronicles the Greater Cincinnati area, exploring 20th and 21st century politics, neighborhood activism, arts organizations, and urban planning. "While a great deal of the material focuses on Cincinnati," says Mr. Grace, "the collection serves as a national case study," providing illuminating research on American urban life and culture.

Acquisitions and Development

Funding for the Archives and Rare Books Library comes mainly through a line budget and through gifts. "There is a small endowment used from time to time, but [outside of the line budget] it's mostly gifts," says Mr. Grace. The endowments the library does receive are relatively small yet range in scope. Mr. Grace explains that there is one endowment strictly for acquiring materials for the Urban Studies Collection, while others are general enough to be used for the acquisition of any rare books. Still, it's an order of business for the library to establish more endowments.

Mr. Grace is solely responsible for acquisition duties at the Archives and Rare Books Library, and while he works within established collection development guidelines, this allows for "relatively all the freedom you need." This holds true for all the UC libraries: "The heads of all the various libraries are considered the selectors, and they just work within their budgets." While Mr. Grace relates that acquisitions have decreased across the board over the last few years, he notes that the overall collections budgets have been preserved over that time period (and have been preserved for some time before that, as well). "[We] haven't really suffered at all," he says. "We've simply redirected funds."

The way the Archives and Rare Books Library's budget has been reduced is such that the library is given a percentage of the line budget, a percentage that has been shrinking. As such, the library has used money to build on strengths rather than expand to other areas. "But things are looking brighter already," adds Mr. Grace. As funds and endowments become available, the focus is to build the Irish literature collection, early travel history, and 18th century British literature.

The library receives about a dozen offers for gifts each year. "We've turned away about as much as we've taken," explains Mr. Grace. "It's a judgment call on each occasion." In this respect, the library is looking for what it does not have, appraising each offer on its pedagogical value to the library's researchers. "With North American Indians [materials], we turn away a lot because we already have a lot. But when it comes to 18th century literature, we take about anything."

Security and Theft

Before the Archives and Rare Books Library was established as a separate entity in 1975, the rare books collection was a victim of renowned book thief Stephen Blumberg, known in library circles as the "Book Bandit." Blumberg was convicted of stealing more than 23,600 rare books and materials from over 250 universities and museums in 45 states, a collection valued at $5.3 million. It was not until Blumberg's arrest in 1990, however, that the University of Cincinnati became aware of its status as one of the Book Bandit's victims.

Still, all this happened prior to the Archives and Rare Books Library's founding, and increased security measures coincided with the library's move: "In 1975, the collection was deemed important enough and valuable enough to have its own dedicated space." In Blegen Library, appropriate doors are alarmed and locked. The stacks themselves are closed, and in terms of shelving and retrieving are accessible by staff only. Standard procedures are in place for registered guests, and the library holds photo I.D. for these patrons. Blegen Library employs a general security staff to cover the entire building, but the Archives and Rare Books Library also maintains a separate security staff for its security purposes alone. While there are no cameras in the reading room due to its unique construction, the library upholds visual security at all times in this area, as well as restricting access to create the most secure environment possible.

Digitization

For about five years now, the library has been actively digitizing its collections. "There were scattered attempts for years before that," says Mr. Grace, "but there's been a concerted effort in the last five years to digitize." The library generally digitizes or scans small items on demand, as per the requests of faculty and students. "Those [requests] come to us almost daily." Mr. Grace regards this as part of the library's regular routine: for example, if a faculty member needs a photograph or a scholarly journal. This work is handled in-house by a dedicated UC library system digitization staff. "Since we're a relatively small operation, we pretty much know what people are requesting," adds Mr. Grace. "But we've also begun to keep formal statistics on these trends."

For larger projects, then, the digitization efforts have been realized through grants, and most of these are completed by outside vendors. This was the case for the digitization of the 530,000 or so Cincinnati birth and death records as part of the Ohio Network Collection. "We keep a running list of what we'd like to digitize," explains Mr. Grace, although oftentimes these desires are dependent on staff. "At this time, we're fulfilling our outstanding grants. But we do keep track of opportunities that arise and see if they fit something on our wish list."

Outreach and Publicity

"Our aim is to make our collections as available as we possibly can," says Mr. Grace, and social media and the internet are vital to this mission. The Archives and Rare Books Library maintains its own website, separate from the general library website, as well as a Facebook page. While the Facebook page is relatively new (it's less than a year old), the library has been actively blogging for years now. "Every time we obtain or catalog a new collection, we blog about it." To get the word out, these blogs get posted on the library's Facebook page, along with the library's website and the general library website.

The Archives and Rare Books Library has at its disposal both the main library's PR department and the university's PR department. "Mostly we use the university's department," says Mr. Grace, citing that they do a better job of contacting local and national media for things like interviews and feature articles. The main library's PR department is useful for its quarterly publications—both print and online—that represent and promote the UC library system. While UC faculty and students comprise the library's primary audience ("We regularly lecture to classes on our holdings," Mr. Grace says, "and we contact those professors teaching courses that could use our collections," adding that the library has had a great deal of success connecting with undergrads), Mr. Grace also emphasizes a need to market to students and scholars outside the university community. "Because we hold government records, we're completely open to the public," explains Mr. Grace. "We're a public library." As such, the library spends a great deal of effort promoting its collections to the general public.

Mr. Grace is also sure to capitalize on assorted public engagements to promote the library as they become available. For example, in January 2013, Mr. Grace spoke at the Sixth World Universities Forum sponsored by the University of British Columbia, presenting his paper titled "University Special Collections from a Global Vantage Point: Access, Documentation and Reference," in which he implores a need to provide context in digitizing to aid teachers, scholars, and students.

The library does not currently have any annual fundraising events marked on its calendar, as time and resources are not available for such occasions. However, it is something that remains on the library's radar. "We definitely want to do those things, it just comes down to the time we have." The library does host a handful of non-fundraising events on a smaller scale, like the monthly "*50 Minutes – 1 Book*" series, a lunchtime talk highlighting a different book from the library's collection each month (recent talks have featured Miguel de Cervantes' *Don Quixote* and Charles Dickens' *Oliver Twist*). The library also regularly invites those scholars conducting research in the collection to present their work to the public, providing a forum for researchers to exhibit their findings.

Exhibits

Exhibit space is readily available to the Archives and Rare Books Library, with display cases in the lobby area of Blegen Library, as well as inside the reading room, in the hallways, and in a large seminar room on the collection's main floor. All this amounts to a regular exhibit schedule. Mr. Grace says there's "no strict schedule," adding that, as with most things, it comes down to time: "We usually rotate these exhibits out quarterly, as we get the time and inclination to do so." The library uses these exhibit spaces to highlight different areas of the collection throughout the year, staggering the schedule so as to be nearly constantly in motion. "Usually whatever we're interested in at the time," says Mr. Grace of the subject matter, noting that currently the library has an exhibit going up that showcases 8,000 digitized images of the abandoned Cincinnati subway system, as well as a exhibit on international buskers. Past exhibits have included highlights from the Arts & Crafts Movement, a Charles Dickens retrospective, and an exploration of Irish Cincinnati.

Preservation

The UC library system as a whole maintains a preservation department—located in the main library—that handles the bulk of the preservation work for the Archives and Rare Books Library. "We meet with them once a month," Mr. Grace says of the preservation department, "and we present three or four individual items we'd like to have preserved or conserved." The selected items are those that Mr. Grace and his staff feel need some extra attention. They tend to choose items that generate the most use, ones that may require a bit more care. He notes that all of the preservation work has been done on rare books. "We haven't had them do anything with archival materials." For some special items, this work is outsourced.

RARE BOOKS AND MANUSCRIPT LIBRARY AT THE OHIO STATE UNIVERSITY

We spoke with Geoffrey D. Smith, Head of the Rare Books and Manuscript Library at The Ohio State University. Mr. Smith has been with the OSU library system since 1983.

General Description

The Rare Books and Manuscript Library (RBMS) exists within the OSU library system under the umbrella of the Special Collections department. Founded as an administrative unit in 1962 (although parts of the collection were already in place before then), RBMS appointed its first curator two years later in Richard Ploch, a then newly-minted Lilly Fellow. Since that time, RBMS has grown into the most expansive of all the umbrella's individual collections, covering disciplines from literature to history, biography to philosophy and more. The collection contains twelfth century medieval manuscripts alongside twenty-first century literary manuscripts, totaling approximately 300,000 volumes of rare books and 2,500 linear feet of manuscripts.

Among the collection's many strengths, Mr. Smith lists the William Charvat Collection of American Fiction as particularly noteworthy, citing it as the strongest research book collection in the OSU system and "one of the outstanding fiction collections in the nation." The Charvat collection boasts approximately 75,000 books from the late eighteenth century to present day. These volumes are further augmented by a strong collection of contemporary American manuscripts from the likes of William S.

Burroughs, Raymond Carver, Frederic Tuten and William T. Vollmann. "[RBMS] is active in developing this portion of the Charvat collection," Mr. Smith adds.

In other areas of traditional scholarship, RBMS was world class collections of Reformation History, Cervantes and Seventeenth-Century English drama. The acquisition of medieval and early modern manuscripts has grown greatly over the past four years under the guidance of Eric J. Johnson in the newly created position, Curator for Medieval and Early Modern Collections.

RBMS also houses a strong Irish collection, focusing on twentieth century authors such as James Joyce and William Butler Yeats and anchored by a healthy collection of Samuel Beckett manuscripts. "We build upon strength," Mr. Smith says, "and Beckett is a strength." Mr. Smith makes sure to add that while the Beckett collection is exceptionally strong, the Joyce collection is formidable as well.

Mr. Smith is especially proud of the Avant Writing Collection, a nascent collection he believes to be already ahead of the game and one he predicts will be a cornerstone of the genre in coming years. "It's an art that has fallen between the cracks of most collections," he explains. "Museums didn't want [these pieces] because they thought of them as text-based, and libraries didn't want them because they thought them art-based." The Avant Writing Collection focuses on pieces that work outside of most standards, pieces most easily thought of as "avant garde," combining both language and art. "Poetry is at the core of this," Mr. Smith says.

The entirety of the RBMS collection is currently housed in three separate locations. The William Oxley Thompson Library, Ohio State's main humanities and social sciences library on campus, is the central home of RBMS and where "the most used and most valuable materials are kept." RBMS also maintains an off-site depository, located in Columbus about fifteen minutes from Thompson Library. This depository, constructed in the Harvard model, contains the most materials among the three locations: RBMS receives two deliveries per day from the depository. The remainder of the collection's materials are stored at a third location, a temporary storage facility that is soon to be taken over by Ohio State's medical school. RBMS is actively looking for a new storage location to take its place when that time comes.

As of just a few years ago, RBMS maintained as many as 6.0 FTE employees, but in recent years this figure has dropped to 4.0 FTE thanks in part to a few select retirements. These numbers do not include the Special Collections cataloging unit, of which there are 6.0 FTE, and while these workers are not exclusive to RBMS, they do provide much assistance. Mr. Smith also cites a healthy budget for student workers.

Acquisitions and Development

The overall RBMS budget comes from university library funding, with an allocation each year for RBMS and a separate budget line, due to its importance, for the Charvat collection. RBMS also receives seven endowments of varying sizes. "They're all very clear as to where the money should go," Mr. Smith says of the endowments, stating that some are for materials only while others cover materials plus operations ("If we want to use it for student funding for a special project," for example). As such, Mr. Smith takes great pride in honoring the intended mission of each bequest, something he feels all institutions should be scrupulous about, particularly with older endowments where donating parties have long since passed.

One endowment of note is the Wing Collection, named after Donald Wing (1904-1972), longtime Associate Librarian at Yale University, whose son Robert Wing is a professor in Ohio State's Astronomy Department. The Wing Collection highlights—exclusively—English literature from 1641 to 1700, or the era revolving around the Glorious Revolution, as was the elder Wing's area of expertise. As such, all endowment monies for the Wing Collection are used to these ends, and Eric Johnson, who administers this fund, is happy to honor these restrictions, thus keeping alive the spirit of the collection.

Mr. Smith happily reports that RBMS is fairly autonomous when it comes to purchasing. "If an article is of a certain value," he explains, "it has to be signed off for. But that's never been an issue." He also relates that RBMS has been fortunate in remaining somewhat status quo over the last few years concerning acquisitions levels, saying they have not received any cuts in this department. In fact, endowments have increased slightly due to a built-in factor guaranteeing the principal does not decrease. "A few years ago we were receiving 5 percent of the endowment. But with recessions, it's been cut down to 3.5 or 4 percent to ensure the principal will continue to grow."

Security and Theft

RBMS hasn't had a serious issue with theft in two decades. "There was an incident going back twenty years or so where two Shakespeare items were stolen," Mr. Smith explains. While the items were ultimately recovered, "it did cause us to reevaluate our security protocol." RBMS has remained in Thompson Library since, but benefited from a $110 million library renovation project completed in 2009. The renovation included state-of-the-art security updates, issuing programmed swipe cards that can assign access levels to all employees and installing a bank of cameras in the reading room. There is also a sizable security staff in Thompson Library, although these guards serve the library on a whole, not just RBMS. Mr. Smith notes that access to rare books is limited to qualified personnel only.

As such, much of the security measures taken by RBMS have been done internally. "We're all security," Mr. Smith offers. "This is something we talk to students about, too." They've updated their sign-in policies, now requiring all visitors to sign in with valid identification, thus ensuring that all visitors are who they say they are. "We had a minor incident years ago where someone signed in with a fake name." But that was an easy fix, as was the policy mandating that two people be on duty at all times, "so no one's ever left alone in the reading room."

Digitization

As with most libraries these days, RBMS is no stranger to the digitization movement. While the library has admittedly been in a transition period, the recent hiring of a Head of Digital Initiatives will incite new projects that involve special collections. RBMS has nonetheless made some modest strides in the digital world. Mr. Smith notes that the library keeps a record of all the scans it makes for patrons. A digital collection celebrating the 400th anniversary of the King James Bible has just been launched, highlighting the library's strong collection of historical bibles. RBMS also hosts a digital text course, where students take manuscripts of journals and diaries and scan them: under the direction of H. Lewis Ulman, Director of the Digital Media Studies department, students have scanned such texts as the letters of Sophia Peabody Hawthorne, Samuel Sullivan Cox's "Journal of a Tour to Europe," and Louisa A. Doane's Journal of Two Ocean Voyages. Still, Mr. Smith predicts that with the hiring of a digital person to spearhead this movement, RBMS's digital efforts will take even more substantial steps forward.

One project Mr. Smith is particularly proud to partner with is the Samuel Beckett Digital Manuscript Project, a collaboration between the University of Antwerp, the University of Reading, and the University of Texas at Austin. On the strength of its Beckett collection, RBMS is "happy to be part of this international initiative," an undertaking that proves to be a serious endeavor, as Mr. Smith estimates it could be twenty-five years before it's all completed.

Outreach and Publicity

"Outreach is an active part of our operations," Mr. Smith remarks, "and we're encouraged more and more to expand our audience." While traditional brochures, newsletters, and visits within the community remain staples of the library's outreach platform, Mr. Smith stresses RBMS's ambition to "encourage youthful excitement with rare books." The library's target audience is skewing younger and younger as the library hopes for increased participation among patrons in their forties, thirties, and even in their twenties. "How can we make [younger people] aware of who we are so that years later, when they think of rare books, they'll think of Ohio State?" In this respect, RBMS is doing more than they've ever done before, much of which Mr. Smith credits to Eric Johnson, Curator of Early Books and Manuscripts. To this end, Mr. Johnson established a Facebook presence for RBMS where there was none before. He also serves as faculty advisor for *De Res*, Ohio State's rare book student organization founded in Fall 2010, a group that includes undergraduate and graduate students alike.

Of course, annual events are major cogs in the library's outreach and fundraising strategies, and Mr. Smith points to two key events on the library's calendar that play vital roles for the sustentation of RBMS. The first is the "Annual Acquisitions Night," where the library presents to the public all the materials added to the collection over the past academic year. This event is held in the library. The second is what's known as "A Tasteful Evening," an annual fundraising night at The Columbus Club that highlights exceptional portions of the RBMS collection, accompanied by an array of "fine tastings."

Such themes in the past have included a sampling of champagnes and bubbly wines and a scotch tasting with an expert scotch master.

Yet aside from these major annual events, it's the everyday efforts that help spread the word beyond just teachers and faculty, and Mr. Smith reiterates a need to "encourage younger participation." There exists an active blogging network among RBMS librarians. The library has also partnered with community groups such as the local bibliophilic society and makes frequent visits to schools to approach younger audiences. A Flickr account has been set up. Mr. Smith also reports that RBMS works closely with the school's Advancement Office (formerly the Development Office), enabling the library to efficiently make contacts and address public groups. Still, some people and groups come to RBMS before RBMS comes to them, either through deliberate action or sheer luck: "Many times there are people who just want to do things with the university," Mr. Smith explains, "and they don't really a place to put it. That's where we come in." When taken in total, it is plain to see that outreach and publicity is a nonstop endeavor, as essential to the livelihood of the collection as the books and manuscripts themselves.

Exhibits

RBMS and the other Ohio State special collections boast a "robust exhibit schedule" says Mr. Smith, presenting roughly three major exhibits a year in the new exhibit hall in Thompson Library. These exhibits are oftentimes booked three or four years in advance. "It's a very visible, very high profile location," Mr. Smith explains of the new and fully secure exhibit space, located in the core of the library. "Anyone in the library system can hold an exhibit there, but Special Collections does tend to do more, because that's what people want to see." He estimates that at least a third of all the exhibits in this space are presented by RBMS. Popular past exhibits, in addition to the King James exhibit mentioned above, have included a Rutherford B. Hayes exhibit, while Mr. Smith is particularly looking forward to an Irish exhibit this fall and a fiftieth anniversary exhibit celebrating the Charvat collection come 2016.

In addition to the main exhibit hall, there is available in the library a large display area consisting of several cases. Unlike the exhibit hall—which sets its own hours—this display area is open as long as the library itself is open. RBMS often takes advantage of this space to show off donations, rotating through the cases a couple times each semester. While the exhibits in these display cases are generally shorter-lived than those in the main exhibit hall, exceptions have been made: last May, for instance, in conjunction with the Sexuality Studies program, RBMS presented to the public a wealth of its LGBT items, an exhibit that lasted several months.

Preservation

For all its book preservation needs, RBMS utilizes the talents of Harry Campbell, full-time Book and Paper Conservator with the OSU library system. Now in his second go-round with Ohio State, Mr. Campbell had been employed for a spell in the 1990s as chief conservator at Etherington Conservation Services in North Carolina but ultimately returned to Ohio State to work with the collections there. Mr. Campbell maintains a healthy staff working under him, operating out of a conservation lab that, while still on campus, is no longer housed at the library: the lab had made its home in the Thompson Library prior to the $110 million renovation project but relocated a few miles away. "The facility itself is outstanding," Mr. Smith remarks, although he readily admits that an off-site lab is not ideal. "Every time you handle a book, every time a book is moved, it's exposed."

MANUSCRIPTS, ARCHIVES, AND RARE BOOK LIBRARY (MARBL), EMORY UNIVERSITY

We spoke with David Faulds, Rare Book Librarian at Emory University's Manuscripts, Archives, and Rare Book Library (MARBL). Mr. Faulds has been with MARBL for eleven years.

General Description

Emory University's Manuscripts, Archives, and Rare Book Library (MARBL) began, as did most rare book collections, from humble beginnings. A number of materials first came to MARBL during the mid-twentieth century—"That's when the first rare book area was set aside," explains Mr. Faulds, although some gift collections also dated back to the 1930s ("Civil War materials," Mr. Faulds says). Still, it wasn't until the late 1960s that MARBL settled into its own dedicated space, and then another decade or so before the collection would experience significant growth, thanks in part to the generosity of one Georgia family.

Founded in 1836, Emory University existed as a small private school for nearly 150 years until an enormous cash gift in 1979 propelled the institution to wealthy university status. Courtesy of an endowment given by Emory's longtime benefactors Robert W. Woodruff (the President of The Coca-Cola Company and active Atlanta philanthropist) and his brother George W. Woodruff, the gift—known as the Emily and Ernest Woodruff Fund—distributed $105 million to the university. At the time of the donation, it was the largest financial gift to an academic institution in the history of the United States. These funds immediately helped stimulate MARBL's growth. "Now we had all these resources to buy materials," says Mr. Faulds. As a result, the library grew by leaps and bounds during the mid to late 1980s, especially developing its Irish literature collection.

Today, MARBL occupies space on two floors of the Robert W. Woodruff Library, Emory's main campus library, with plans to expand to a third floor by February 2013. "The entire book collection will be in one place," says Mr. Faulds of the move, "rather than on two floors." The library is best known for its modern English language literature collection and its African American collection. "Those are the two areas we promote the most, where most of our money goes." The former boasts an impressive lineup including Ted Hughes, Salman Rushdie, Alice Walker, and Seamus Heaney. The latter is broader in scope, with emphasis on the following principal areas: the Freedom Struggle's Leaders and Organizations; Black Print Culture; Blacks and the Left; African American Literature and the Arts; and Expatriate Literary and Cultural Figures. Highlights include the papers of the Southern Christian Leadership Conference and the library of Carter G. Woodson. MARBL also maintains a healthy collection of materials relating to Southern history, with a particular focus on Georgia and Atlanta. When all is said and done, Mr. Faulds estimates the collection houses several hundred thousand volumes, but emphasizes that this figure is an estimate since the process of tallying the collection is an ongoing process.

Acquisitions and Development

"We would like to build our endowments," explains Mr. Faulds. "That's where we have to grow." As a relatively young collection—at least compared to the likes of Harvard and Yale—MARBL's endowments are modest in scope, although the collection is "lucky to have the support of both library administration and university administration." These endowments, as such, supplement the overall funding from the university and the library itself. "That's where a lot of support comes from," Mr. Faulds says of the administrations.

MARBL's acquisitions department, as described by Mr. Faulds, maintains a high level of independence. Those endowments that do stipulate how endowed monies should be spent are relatively small, whereas the broader endowments can be used at MARBL's discretion. The curatorial staff handling all acquisitions consists of five library personnel: two curators for the African American collection, one curator for the literary collection, and a fourth curator for the Southern Historical collection. The last spot belongs to Mr. Faulds, who cites his influence to be "not as much as that of the others" in this respect.

As the library has been able to catalog its acquisitions over the last ten years, in a sense playing catch-up in tallying the good amount of donations and additions received during that time (Mr. Faulds especially points to the acquisition of the Raymond Danowski Poetry Library in 2004, with its 75,000 volumes of modern and contemporary poetry along with tens of thousands of periodicals, as a sudden tax on inventory), the acquisitions team has been able to increase steadily its overall additions. Says Mr. Faulds: "[We've] been able to work out what we don't have and what we do have. It's helped to get a better handle on what we already own." He cites the recent hiring of the Southern Historical collections curator and a second African American collections curator to be keys to overall increased acquisitions. "We're also getting more gifts, particularly in the African American collection."

Security and Theft

Woodruff Library security is on-site twenty-four hours a day, serving not just MARBL but the entire library as a whole. As a result of MARBL's recent growth, stronger security measures have been put in place to bring the library up to the level of recommended guidelines and that of their peer institutions. Cameras are positioned strategically in the reading room, and overall reading room rules have tightened, placing restrictions on the bringing in outside materials. MARBL is also conducting a review of security procedures in conjunction with the move into their new space one level below. This will include a revamping of the main floor where the reading room is located, introducing new security measures ("There will be zero public access to the new floor") and issuing access cards on all floors.

Digitization

For a few years now, MARBL has been making strides with digitization, utilizing a Kirtas mass-digitizing machine. "[The machine] is slightly older now," explains Mr. Faulds, "but it's done good work for us." While the library hasn't done much with its manuscript collections just yet, the plan is to move in that direction, starting with the Robert Langmuir African American Photograph Collection, the library's first large-scale manuscript collection to be digitized. However the collection, which was sent off-site to be digitized, represents a unique challenge for MARBL's digitization efforts: as with the library's twentieth century literature collection, much of the African American collection cannot be digitized due to copyright restrictions. In fact, much of what has been digitized is simply a product of what can be digitized. "In the past," says Mr. Faulds, "we've been working with books and looking for groups of books where we have a significant amount of material." The result is that the library has done a lot of nineteenth century British literature, in addition to some materials from its African American collection—but again only where the documents are out of copyright and are in good enough condition to be digitized.

Still, in an attempt to eliminate those gray areas between what's forbidden and what's allowed, the photograph collection project is proving to be an impetus for establishing more definitive rules at MARBL regarding copyright restrictions, thus paving the way for a stout future of digitization at MARBL. This shift toward digitization is reflected in MARBL's staff as well, with the hiring of a new Director (Rosemary Magee) and a new Senior Vice Provost for Library Services and Digital Scholarship (Rich Mendola), both of whom came from within the library.

On the manuscript side of things, MARBL employs two archivists to handle the born-digital and electronic archives, something Emory has been known for for years. Mr.

Faulds adds that MARBL continues to work strongly in this department. Of especial interest is the library's collection of Salman Rushdie's personal computers, four in all, the acquisition of which marked the first time the library had acquired a complete computing environment. Access to Rushdie's digital archives is available via a dedicated research workstation in the reading room which allows researchers to browse the entire processed collection while replicating the original computing experience. To date, it is MARBL's most complete set of born-digital records.

Also of note is MARBL's "Re-Mapping Segregated Atlanta" collaboration, a digital research project utilizing rare maps and manuscript collections to facilitate study of Jim Crow Atlanta. The project maps data in a geographic information system (GIS), a system designed to capture, store, manipulate, and manage geographically-referenced data. As per the project's website: "It is difficult to analyze segregation because much of its physical history has disappeared from the contemporary city's landscape. ... 'Re-Mapping Segregated Atlanta' develops tools to visualize and analyze segregation's imprint on the city by creating new ways to integrate spatial and non-spatial data into research and the classroom." This interdisciplinary initiative draws upon the skills of librarians from across the Emory Libraries system.

Outreach and Publicity

MARBL maintains a webpage on the main Emory Libraries site, which is currently undergoing the process of moving platforms. Mr. Faulds sees this as a great opportunity to overhaul the MARBL page, a time to revise content, a time to expand. The library's online presence has already grown significantly since the hire of a new staff reference librarian, with a regularly-updated blog and a new Facebook profile among the chief tools used.

There exists a PR department within Woodruff Library, and while this department is not exclusive to MARBL, the two do work together often. "We have a development office there for outreach, consisting of two staff members," says Mr. Faulds. As part of its outreach efforts, MARBL issues a print publication promoting the collection (about ten pages long, similar to a magazine) every six months or so. The main arm of MARBL's outreach, however, is MARBL's wide array of public events. Citing an influx of new and enthusiastic curatorial staff members as a driving force behind the library's lively events schedule, Mr. Faulds points to two fundraisers in particular which greatly boost the collection's profile: one event showcasing the library's literary collection, another showcasing the African American collection. The latter is typically held at a local supporter's residence and features the sale of a unique print produced by an African American artist, exclusively for purposes of increasing the endowment. The fundraiser for the literary collection is a highlight of the events calendar, as each year MARBL invites a poet to speak and read. Past speakers have included such luminaries as U.S. Poet Laureates Robert Pinsky and Billy Collins and Pulitzer Prize winner Mary Oliver. Mr. Faulds is especially excited for upcoming speakers Seamus Heaney (a Nobel laureate) and Natasha Trethewey, Director of the Creative Writing Program at Emory and, as of September 2012, the current U.S. Poet Laureate.

In addition to these heavy-hitting literary events, MARBL is proud to present the Raymond Danowski Poetry Library Reading Series. Free and open to the public, this reading series features two or three poets each year, including Sonia Sanchez, Simon Armitage, Lucille Clifton, and Galway Kinnell. In all, MARBL events maintain a consistent influx of talent—thanks in large part to Kevin Young, Curator of Literary Collections and the Raymond Danowski Poetry Library. Mr. Young, a poet himself and recent finalist for the 2013 National Book Critics Circle Award for his first book of criticism, "The Grey Album: On the Blackness of Blackness," is "well connected" in the poetry world, notes Mr. Faulds. "He's great at bringing in speakers."

Exhibits

MARBL has access to a few exhibition spaces in Woodruff Library and takes advantage of these spaces to present about three exhibits each year. The main exhibit space resides on the second floor of the library. "That's pretty much always MARBL materials," says Mr. Faulds, noting that these exhibits get changed out once or twice a year. Past exhibits here have included highlights from the acquisitions of Alice Walker and Salman Rushdie ("Both writers showed up for their openings, and Christopher Hitchens was on hand for Rushdie's as well" adds Mr. Faulds). But there are also options for smaller, short-term exhibits scattered throughout the library, with a few cases in the entryway, for example, or up on the tenth floor. These exhibits generally last only a few months before they are rotated out. With a range of options available for display purposes, Woodruff Library dedicates three staff positions to exhibition planning.

Preservation

Preservation for MARBL is handled on-site on the first floor of Woodruff Library. "Every now and then something will be sent off-site that the lab cannot do," Mr. Faulds says, "but mostly it's all in-house." He recalls one grant-funded project in particular where the preservation duties were outsourced. The lab employs three staff conservation members, and as the lab has grown quite a bit, it's physically at its capacity. "The challenge is space. It simply takes up a lot of room." As such, MARBL is actively looking at options to expand its preservation space. Mr. Faulds adds that digital preservation is going to be a focus, too.

A POSTSCRIPT ON THE EFFORTS OF LAW ENFORCEMENT AGENCIES IN COMBATING RARE BOOK AND DOCUMENT THEFT

In the eyes of many law enforcement officials, rare book and document theft is far more common than generally believed. Rare book collections are often inadequately cataloged, and even library general collections often contain rare volumes that have simply been improperly cataloged or miscataloged as general collection items rather than the rare gold that they are. Moreover, unlike other forms of cultural intellectual property, such as paintings of sculpture, pieces or segments from rare books are often very valuable as stand alone items themselves even when separated from the main work. Maps, illustrations, drawings, photographs, poems, short stories, even dust jackets, have value as stand alone items – and this encourages the facile thief who may be able to make a getaway with a few choice pages clipped from a Gutenberg Bible or classic 19th century civil war photos. At least until recently, directors of rare book divisions may have – if not looked the other way, at least not pressed for investigations of missing pages or works, and sometimes may not have even known that they were missing. Moreover, while many prominent rare book collections have ample endowments for acquisitions, the special security equipment and staff needed for proper security often have to be paid for straight out of stressed university or public library or foundation budgets. Most great rare book collections are under the auspices of universities, not institutions known for their great dedication to internal security. In many cases, at least in North America, local police leave most elements of policing up to campus security forces, more skilled in shepherding inebriated students back to their dorm rooms than protecting or tracking down filched first editions of *Tom Sawyer*.

Stolen books also seem to have a greater chance of eluding detection on the commercial market than other forms of stolen intellectual or cultural property. Although screening and alert systems have improved, according to those interviewed for this report, they are still inadequate. According to the Museum Security Network, a Dutch-based organization (as cited in the Schneier Security blog, 3/20/09), only 2% to 5% of rare book thefts are recovered vs. 50% of thefts of artwork. The website of the museum security network is: http://www.museum-security.org/.

The rudiments of a security grapevine are in place. The International League of Antiquarian Booksellers maintains a website www.stolen-books.org which has a database of items reported stolen after June 15, 2010, and some additional information on books stolen prior to that date. Unfortunately the website has no shortage of thefts. A quick check of the site in October 2012 revealed details of more than 1,600 thefts from all over the world.

The organization's website explains that: "The League and its national associations has a long history of preventing book theft and of catching book thieves, both at national and international level. This also applies to stolen maps as well as documents, manuscripts and other related material. We work closely with booksellers, libraries, museums, the police, national governments and other interested bodies. Our intention is that thieves will have nowhere to dispose of their ill gotten goods."

The Rare Book and Manuscript Division of the Association of College and Research Libraries, a division of the American Library Association, also maintains a website that lists monthly thefts of rare books and manuscripts.

The FBI maintains a National Stolen Art File and this database also covers other cultural objects such as books and manuscripts. The database of stolen rare books can be searched as one of the search options from the following website: http://www.fbi.gov/about-us/investigate/vc_majorthefts/arttheft

The general book category can be searched and the search can also be refined by title, period or other criteria.

The United Kingdom has a useful site called FindStolenArt which can be reached at: http://www.findstolenart.com. The database can be searched specifically for rare books.

The growth of Ebay and other auction sites, as well as Amazon and other online book dealers, have made it easier to quickly dispose of stolen rare books, documents and photographs before they are known to be missing.

The way that rare book and document theft is viewed by the public is also a factor in its profusion. Rare book thieves are often depicted in the popular press, and in books, as something like eccentric, wayward, if ultimately lovable uncles, who perhaps drink a little too much. Certainly this type of thief exists but the high returns of filched books, and particularly prints, photographs and other items that can be easily cut out and not easily traced, has encouraged an entirely larger class of moonlighting thief and drawn professional criminals. According to some law enforcement officials, two thirds of rare book thefts are not by library patrons but by library employees or other insiders with off-hours access to the library.

Some of the most dramatic cases of rare book theft involve thieves that stole literally hundreds of times, often from the same libraries over and over. It is this characteristic of repeated theft, often literally under the nose of library administrators, and frequently involving either library insiders, or trusted practitioners of the rare books trade, that so often shames librarians and sometimes leads them to prosecute such crimes with less enthusiasm than many would like. One of the most egregious cases was the case of Farhad Hakimzadeh, an Iranian businessman who became infamous for cutting out pages from book in the British Library and Oxford University Library, and using them to enhance the value of his existing personal collection. Hakimzadeh actually ran a publishing company that specialized in books about the Middle East, and fancied himself something of an ambassador of Iranian culture. According to British press reports, Hakimzadeh used a scalpel and reportedly only chose books from which missing pages would be difficult for non-experts to detect. He received a two year prison sentence from

British courts which seems a relatively light sentence for someone who reportedly stole elements from 150 books over a 5-year period. He was also ordered to pay court costs of about $11,000.

Hakimzadeh is a wealthy individual who lived in a $4 million home in an upscale London neighborhood. In addition to the criminal charges, the British Library sued him for 300,000 pounds in damages (about $450,000). He was also ordered to pay court costs of about $11,000. A press report in the British newspaper The Guardian suggests that this was the second time around for Hakimzadeh, saying that in 1998 he had paid 75,000 pounds in compensation to the Royal Asiatic Society for thefts from that institution.

The British Library requires identification for a patron to view a rare book and keeps records of the identities of those viewing particular items; they reviewed all 842 items that he had requested to see and established the pattern of mutilation and theft.

Other such thefts by prominent collectors and others thought beyond reproach have led to a rethinking of security issues in the rare book world that have significantly impacted scholarly collections and how they are housed, maintained and secured.

www.ingramcontent.com/pod-product-compliance
Lightning Source LLC
Chambersburg PA
CBHW080846020526
44114CB00045B/2680